To the dreamer in each of us,

THANK GOD I'M FIRED

A CORPORATE ENIGMA

SANDEEP PAWAR

INVINCIBLE PUBLISHERS

First Printing: 2019

ISBN: 978-93-89600-05-6

Invincible Publishers

Registered Address: 201A, SAS Tower, Sector 38, Gurgaon - 122003

Baba,
I miss you.

NOTE TO THE READERS

This book by no way asks you to hate your job or particularly your boss. Neither does it intend to add fuel if you already do so nor does it take the responsibility if you want to punch the boss in the face and leave the job like a boss. Don't make this cute book a partner in your cold-blooded crime.

However, if you yourself are a boss then remember this book is a work of fiction and the characters and events are solely imaginative. Bosses are nice and you know that, I know.

Instead, after reading this book, you may become the best version of yourself. You will start loving your job and wait for Monday morning from Friday evening.

Ah, just kidding.

This book does not claim to be an account of facts and events but more of personal experiences, the experiences of acquaintances, and the professional folklores. It tries to address the inside dilemmas of professionals and intends to be of little help in striving for their inner calling. Sweet intention, isn't it?

Before opening the real show, I wish to say this sincerely- Thank you for picking up this book. I must say you've got a great choice. Seriously you do. Now buckle up and get ready for the quick ride. Here we go!

PROLOGUE

I boarded a shared cab on my way to Whitefield and witnessed an unusual creature sitting beside me- no office wares and no ID card hanging. Maybe it was the first time that I was sharing a cab heading towards the IT hub with a non-IT person. Is that even possible? This is Bangalore after all. Five minutes into it and our cab got stuck into another traffic jam. As a norm, a gush of irritation spread all over the road. But the guy beside me did not seem to be irritated. Was he traffic-immortal? That made me more curious about him. Who was he? God? Where was he going wearing shorts on Tuesday morning?

Every cloud has a silver lining, even Bangalore traffic has. Traffic is the best excuse any Bangalorian could try and I bet they'll never fail to manipulate their bosses about the late coming. People stuck in traffic jams tend to talk with other stuck souls to bash the traffic together and vent out their frustration. So in a way, traffic jams are letting people come closer- both by bodies and most importantly by hearts.

After a full minute into the jam, my curiosity started exploding inside.

"It's a regular thing. Nowadays if I don't get stuck in a jam, I feel like I'm travelling in the parallel world. This city is flooding with software folks. They should not be allowed anymore. Can't they see the house-full board? Go elsewhere, folks." I blabbered making eye contact with the creature.

He just nodded with a smile. He wasn't impressed with the idea of banning software tribes to the city. Who was he? A quintessential corporate social worker?

"Aren't you into a software job?" I asked although it was none of my business.

I like stranger talks. It is my hobby. It is even mentioned in my resume.

"I used to." Finally, he parted his lips, keeping his mobile back to his pocket. From his body language, I suspected he was getting ready for the conversation. Bang on! His one eye was on the jam though.

"Where are you heading then?" I asked looking outside the window pretending it was a casual question.

"For a movie."

"Which one?"

"Ah, nothing is planned. This is so instantaneous and unplanned plan." He said and extended his hand- "Raghav,"

After a momentous handshake, I diverted the conversation to my main topic of interest- his job.

"What did you say about the job?"

"I used to, I said." He was as steady as the vehicles in the traffic jam. Why was he so cold headed?

"Used to? Not anymore? Following a passion or what?" I commented sarcastically to regret only a moment later. Was it too personal after meeting a stranger for mere five minutes?

He laughed. "You can say that."

"Read tonnes of self-help books and left the job or what?" I wanted to know why he was not into software despite being young and in Bangalore. I was being impatient. Maybe regular traffic jams make you that way.

"You really want to know?" He asked with a tinge of hope in his eyes.

Maybe he had no one to listen to his stories. Don't worry, stranger. I-will-be-there-for-you.

"I am always open to such stories. But don't drag. And don't brag." I ordered as if I was his angel investor and he was about to make his elevator pitch.

"Ah! Don't worry. Till this jam gets clear, my story would be over. I bet."

"People sitting all day for hours looking at a glowing light are bound to get run over like a deer in headlights."

- **Richie Norton**

Yesterday

1

Sometimes, you get a feeling from within and can sense immediately if something is wrong, even if there is no clear reason. Today, I am sensing such feeling. It may be due to Monday blues or maybe it's just my superstitious mind as my right eye is twitching constantly. I'm not sure whether the latter is a good or bad omen but with these thoughts, I am getting ready for work. The work which doesn't work for me. Just to tell you, today is not any other ordinary day; it is a crucial, decisive day of my life. I'm going to start a new chapter by closing one, the consequences of which are not very clear, at least to me. I'm nervous, and the uncalled interim feeling is making me more nervous.

I reached the office a bit late, thirty minutes to be exact. Although it says flexible working hours, a deceptive term to catch the fishes, a few cohorts stare as if I was responsible for their bad moods. I ignored them. That's the ultimate option I had. Immediately, I went to my desk.

It was a start of the week with two whole days of holidays, but even after that people's faces were dull and tired. There wasn't a trace of excitement. No doubt Monday is cursed. No one loves it and it is probably the most hateful nonliving thing. It must've done some terrible business in its past life. But still it didn't learn any lesson and repeating the same in its current life. Monday in corporate office feels like a graveyard and rightfully so, they say- on Mondays, employees don't come to the office, their corpses do. Our firm had found a sympathiser for it- Monday Musings. It is this short tale often with a morale copied from some website. Like any other HR emails, employees don't hesitate to ignore it and trash it as soon as it pops up.

But as I'm unique, I read it.

"Do you really read it?" Once Ravi, my teammate, asked me surprisingly when he was secretly gaping my screen.

"Yes, I do."

His mouth was wide open as if it was a crime to read HR's emails.

"Oh God. So this makes you the only person reading it. I bet these HRs too don't read it before sending. Once they had copied only half and abruptly ended mid-word. Can you believe, mid-word?"

I knew he eavesdrop my conversation and secretly watch my monitor as if it's every neighbour's birthright. He puts on headphones and pretend as if he is listening to something on it whenever I talk with other people. I was suspicious and kept a close eye on him to find out that once he did not even connect his headphones to any device. I did not say anything to him because I know how irresistible it is to not hear to or look into other's business. Another reason of not confronting him was,

I was also a culprit in the same crime just my ways were different.

I opened the Monday Musing and started reading it.

Happiness Carrot

Two rabbits, Joy and Joe, were working for Jimmy, a fox. Joy and Joe used to work sincerely for Jimmy and in return he used to give them carrots, their favorite food.

"Two carrots a day. Work for six days and Sunday is off. If you please me, you will get bonus carrots for Sunday because I am cute. And that's the deal." Jimmy had clarified on the first day for which both the rabbits agreed happily.

"I am happy as Sunday is off and I can practice guitar on Sunday." Joy told Joe.

"But what about the future? We shall work on Sundays too and secure more and more carrots and thus the future." Joe protested.

Soon after Joe started working on Sundays and started getting more carrots while as Joy learnt playing guitar wonderfully. Joe became Jimmy's favorite as he worked throughout the week for his business and he started giving him incentives. Joe started earning double than Joy.

"Take some rest my friend. See at your health. It is deteriorating." Joy advised.

"You need not worry about it. Have you seen how much carrots I have?" Joe denied.

The years went by. Joy became professional guitarist and happily performed everywhere. Joe became the richest rabbit in town but need to visit every type of doctor all the while. Once when he was lying on dentist's table, he heard Joy playing guitar on the radio. He asked himself- 'Who is more successful?'

It made me think profusely. If employees read such stories, they would be motivated to start doing what they like and most of them would leave their jobs. I thought Ravi was correct- even HRs didn't read what they write to all.

The moment I realized what my real agenda for the day was, I immediately stopped thinking about the musing. I typed my heart out- an important email, a very important email indeed. The email I should have sent months back, I thought. But better late than never. I typed it at lightning speed. I had practiced it a thousand times in my head- word by word. My heart pounded every time I read it, again and again. My mind asked for its sanity. Was I insane? Was I an emotional fool? But this time, I was determined not to give a second thought and waste time; I'd had enough of it. Just before I hit the send button and give a full stop to all the bewildering chaos, my phone rang. Why phones ring at wrong times?

"Good morning, Raghav. It's Harish here." The known voice, an unpleasant one.

"Good morning, Harish."

"Please come to Anemone; we need to discuss something important."

"Sure," I assured.

I am not sure why they name meeting rooms with such fancy names which no one understands or can correctly pronounce. I sensed something unusual, two things in particular. My manager, Harish, doesn't come to the office so early, and if he wants to discuss something, he calls for a meeting in his office and not in some fancy, flowery named room. But today was different. Immediately, I got up from my seat. In the dilemma of when to send my ready-to-send email to Harish, I decided to see him first. I poured some strong coffee to digest his bitter words. What would he speak about apart from agile, responsibility, ownership, audits and similar jargon? I knew what was in store for me there. But today I didn't care much.

On my way, a girl in her business formals caught my attention. She was waiting outside Amaryllis, our interview room. While walking past her, a thought emerged.

'Don't come here. Don't join. It's a trap. Look at me. Oh dear, look at me. Say no to them.' I wanted to scream at her. I stopped for a moment. 'Wait. She must be knowing this. After working in corporates, who doesn't know about corporates? No organization is different. It's just us who hop with a hope that probably this organization would be different in a good sense. This hope is responsible for everything.' I walked away silently. Who knows she could become an exception? I didn't want to break her hope. Why would I when Morgan Freeman himself advised in Shawshank Redemption- 'Hope is a good thing, maybe the best of things'?

With my cup, I entered the meeting room to witness my next shock. Suchi, the HR manager, was engrossed in a serious conversation, standing next to Harish. Your manager along with HR is always a deadly combination. As soon as I entered, they stopped their whispering immediately. What were they discussing? Nuclear deal?

"Good morning, Raghav, please have a seat." Suchi was in her typical HR avatar.

"Good morning," I greeted too.

Neither she nor I meant any good morning to each other. But, corporate etiquette.

Harish was silent, like a criminal. He too had a cup of tea- office's free green tea. We both looked at each other's cups- He at my coffee cup and I at his green tea cup. I could see envy in his eyes for my sugared coffee. I had no such feelings for him or his drink. I wonder if they won't get green tea for free, would they anytime drink it. Maybe not. Never.

Suchi took the pilot seat and started driving the meeting.

"So, Raghav, how are you doing?" Still in her HR mode.

"Good," I answered without asking about her. I was in a typical employee mode.

Harish was still silent. Typical manager mode when he is supposed to take a stance.

"So, you must be aware of our company's situation, especially about this office."

I didn't care about either of them.

"Yes, yes," I muttered without having much idea. We all are liars.

"Unfortunately, we don't have an option but to sack a few valuable employees from our office too," she continued, a little awkwardly.

I was getting a feeling where this was going. I chose not to react. I put on a stone face mask. My poker skills helped. I looked straight in her eyes. She held those down. I repeated the same with Harish. He followed her actions.

'Then why the hell are you hiring that beauty?' I wanted to scream at them. But that was not going to help, I knew. Because for every sane question, they had the insane answer- it's a management decision. This decision making authority is always sneaky and invisible. No one knows where this management resides and no one has seen them either.

The room had become so quiet that you could hear a pin drop in the silence. I couldn't get enough of what she was trying to convey but sensed something fishy. With enough awareness of the industry, I brought down the dead silence to three possibilities: either I was sacked, or Harish was, or we both were. After an awkward half a minute, Harish came forward. He looked determined. From his body language, I rubbed out the last two possibilities.

"So, Raghav, we know and fully understand you are an important resource for us," he started with a lie. I wanted to laugh out loud.

If all managers competed in a lying contest, Harish would top the chart. Who would come after him? The question made me think.

"But sadly, the management has decided to release you. This is very unfortunate for us, but this is clearly a management decision, and we must sadly abide by it. I hope you understand. It is a very difficult situation, undoubtedly more for you we understand, but some decisions are out of our hands." He continued placidly as if he had already rehearsed the speech for a week.

I was stunned and frozen. Unknowingly, anguished expressions appeared on my face. I was unable to think and comprehend what was happening. I couldn't match his eyes. I looked around to get some better sight. The room was decorated with a lot of corporate posters. In those posters, there were happy, jaw-dropping gorgeous people, perfectly groomed and tucked in suits and smiling as if they had their dream jobs. If that was less dramatic, quotes accompanied them. The whole thing must be from an alternate reality where employers and employees are in mutually enriching relationship. There was more love for the work than the newly wed couple on the honeymoon.

"Have a glass of water, Raghav," Suchi offered me a glass and halted my train of thought.

Definitely, she'd come prepared, otherwise who keeps the glass ready? I took a sip, happy that I had a glass to stare at until they both completed their speeches.

"I know this must be a tremendous shock for you, and we also feel very bad about this decision. But you know how certain things in life are beyond our control, and we should see the..."

She continued, but after her few repetitive words, my ears had automatically stopped catching her dialogue. I was fully concentrating on the glass. How beautifully crafted it was!

"So as company policy, you are entitled to a compensation package..."

Suddenly, my antenna started catching those words. Did she just say 'compensation'?

Compensation is the key to happiness.

"As you will be relieved immediately, you will get two month's salary. After the meeting, please come to my office, and we'll go through the formalities. We are again sorry, but we are left with no other choice."

I thought the speech was over. But I was wrong. She was in full mood to make me more embarrassed.

"Are you okay, Raghav?" She continued with the most obvious question.

Who doesn't answer 'yes' to such questions?

"Yes, I'm okay," I answered in the most obvious and dull way. Honestly, I was relieved and probably the happiest person in Anemone. I was slowly realizing the latter part and that was making me happy. But I need not to show it. Was that only through sheer serendipity that I got fired?

"Good. Let's move on, and all the very best. I know, of course, you'll do great in future. See you in the office in ten minutes. We need to go through a non-disclosive closure agreement and that's all." She tapped my shoulder in consolidation, and they both prepared to leave.

A flood of emotions ran through my mind.

Did she say agreement? Did I have any say in that agreement? I knew the answer. It was of course- No. Agreements have to be two-sided, aren't they? But corporate agreements are different; often employer forces their mandates and employees have to agree to it and they agree to call it an agreement. Sweet.

Was I fired? Could I be fired? Really? Once a topper of the class, could I be fired? My senses turned numb in disbelief. The biggest misconception I had about myself that I was a job-immortal was broken. We live in delusions. There are certain situations we think we would never be in. For me, getting sacked from the job was one of them. What misconception tops the list? Well, getting me malaria maybe? Why would a rare female Anopheles search me among thousands of people and bite me? Am I that unique and unlucky at the same time? But what happened some time back in Anemone forced me to rub down the never-happening-with-me list from my mind.

Sitting there alone, I couldn't keep the news just to myself for long. Such news is too tough to hold off. How solely only one small mind could keep it? The first name that came to my mind to break the news was, without any doubt, Indu.

"I have news," I blurted over the phone.

"Finally! Did you resign?" Within no time, she'd guessed.

"No. They did not even give me that chance."

"Chance? What do you mean?"

"Instead, they fired me."

"What?"

"Yes, they did."

"So, no notice period?" She asked.

"Not a single day."

"So relieved, aren't you?"

"There is something more. They offered me a compensation package too- two months' salary."

There was a hushed silence.

"Congratulations man!" She screamed happily as if that was the best possible thing that could happen to me. Maybe it really was.

"And more for getting fired on Monday." She continued.

"Why so?"

"Dude, you're getting weekend's salary as well. If you had been fired on Friday, you must've lost two days salary. Always remember one thing."

"What's that?"

"Join the company on Friday and leave it on Monday."

I completed the formalities without uttering a word to Suchi and without showing a pinch of happiness on my face. I went to my desk and collected all the useful things, cleared the clutter and did the most important thing-deleted the resignation email I'd drafted in the morning.

That was my third attempt from the past week to have the resignation email ready but not sent. And today too, fortunately, I failed, but for all the right reasons. Some failures win you the game. Sometimes, when you can't do what you want, destiny does it for you.

I reached my desk and started rummaging in haste. I leaned over and opened the drawer and in the litter of chocolate wrappers, I saw the badge. My 'Employee of the month' badge. I laughed seeing my smiling photo on it. For a minute, it got me confused whether the badge should be considered as litter. Aren't such badges a mere covering just like those wrappers? They make sure employees stay away from the real intentions of these employers. Not to be overdramatic, I kept it in my bag. I looked at the board and there was Puru smiling, just like me. It was his turn to be an 'Employee of the month'. Would he too get fired like me in future? And most importantly, if he does, would he be lucky and happy like me?

I glanced around. It seemed like a normal, usual working day for everybody else. People were in their own worlds. Humans are unpredictable. They hide ruckus of emotional turmoil behind their composed faces. I was doing the same. Everyone must be struggling with their unique set of problems, I thought. And for them, theirs is the biggest problem. They are hardly bothered by other's problems. We all are the same. It's human nature. 'It's going to be okay because it's not happening to you' I had read somewhere and remembering it, I had a smile. Looking at all those folks, I wondered- Would they ever miss me? At the least, remember me? Then I asked the same question to myself about them. I had no clear answer.

The show must go on. And it goes on- with you or without you.

Our office boy Vinod, a good friend of mine, was passing by.

"Badhiya?" He asked with a smile as he used to ask me every day, and quickly ran towards the pantry. Like every day he did not wait for my answer. And why would he wait? After all, Vinod is the busiest man in the office.

"Badhiya," I muttered, not sure whether I was speaking the truth.

The sound of keyboard thumping, those giggles, continuous telephone rings, stand up meetings, and all such office turbulence, I was witnessing for the last time probably. On the emotional and sentimental front, I would definitely miss the good time I spent in the workplace, but I couldn't stick to this work for a lifetime, maybe where I didn't even belong. Someone once wisely said, 'If you want to reach somewhere, you need to leave from somewhere.'

When It All Started

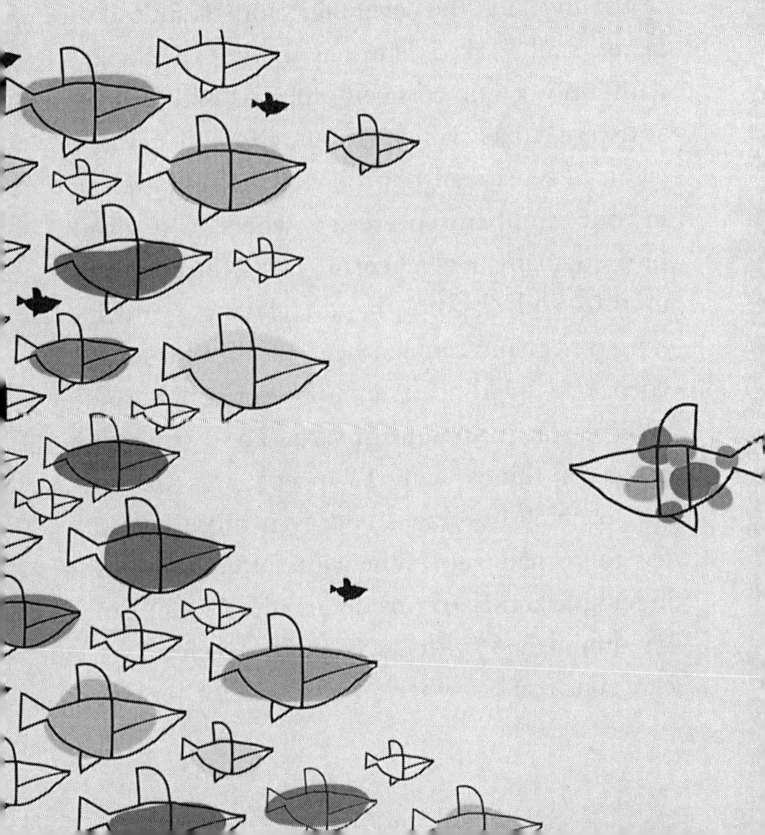

2

It's five in the evening, and Kamlesh's tea stall looked like a gathering. A social gathering- a fair of lively, spirited and happy software folks which is an altogether rare sight. His tea stall is probably the only place in our company premises where you can find so many real cheerful faces, blabbering mouths and clapping hands. Having a small, not so hygienic canteen near an ultra-hygienic corporate building is an unprescribed norm. The reason is straightforward. The two most common things with IT peeps are- hatred for machine beverages and even more hatred for their managers. When the latter hatred is inevitable and also considerate, the former can be diminished with such stalls. 'Technology can take you anywhere, but it cannot replace the human touch,' my professor used to say, which we used to repeat in group discussions for bashing technology. It worked pretty well every time. And when I jumped into the corporate world years back, it felt exactly true, at least for beverages. The short stroll for tea is the most refreshing time of the day. Witnessing the crowd lingering near the tea stalls, waiting for their turn, chit-chatting, sharing cigarettes; it is irresistible not to think about opening a tea-startup.

"We'll earn at least a lakh every month." Puru, another entrepreneurship aspirant colleague, assured me one day. "See. We can office-deliver teas. The concept is simple and unique, office-doorstep-tea. See. Let's suppose we get at least ten offices initially. Fifty teas per office. Five hundred teas every evening. Five rupees profit every tea. So, it comes to around seventy-five thousand just from the evening. Add morning, and we can earn at least a lakh. You see?" He continued taking the last sip. "And we shall convince people that green tea doesn't help to reduce fats. It just burns the money."

I haven't heard such absurd and groundless calculations. What surprises me more about Puru is that one day he will talk about his tea-startup and making me a partner in that, and the very next day he won't utter a word about it. Again, after a month or so, he will make the same point and put the same calculations in my plate. Later, when I observed the pattern carefully, I concluded that when he used to get bashed by his boss, he'd come to his startup and the next day he forgot about both- the bashing from the boss and the startup. He even thought about the name of the venture– 'Teaster' as a tribute to the unsung heroes of the industry- the testers.

~

My team of six, all men unfortunately, was regular and always on time to Kamlesh. It was the only time when no one, especially our fluffy faced boss, was behind us. It felt like freedom, although just for half an hour. Kamlesh now feels like a family. The only worst part of this visit was- leaving.

The open sky with sun striking hard on us feels more satisfying than full-blown ACs. The scene is always pleasing with boiling tea spreading its aroma and people enjoying it with spiced up discussions. The discussions range from movies, cricket, politics to what the boss said during one-on-one confidential meetings, which are always entertaining to be part of. While most of these talks are lightweight and stress busters, some are very funny and ironic. You could even see smokers talking about pollution, environmental conservation, and passive smokers pretending to listen to them to conserve the friendships. You could witness the people talking about drought in the villages and saving water who had flushed liters of water unnecessarily some time back and would do so again.

After the washrooms, there are tea stalls well-reserved for frank discussions. If you are well-versed in eavesdropping, you'll listen to the interesting stories which are often the gossips about their colleagues and proving how their boss is a douchebag. But there comes a day or two when these folks spit out their fears.

What could be the deadliest fear than getting sacked from the job? Isn't it the dirtiest stain they could feel on their white collared job?

"Then he said- okay, I understand the situation, and the best I can do is, I will send my resignation today to Reema, my reporting HR. And guys, you know what happened next?" Prakash was explaining yet another case of firing in the IT industry over tea. I hadn't seen him so excited anytime earlier and also everyone around him. There was so much devotion, so much interest in the group. Firing is a topic that brings tremendous excitement among the audience, of course, when you are not the one who got fired.

"What?" The eager group shouted in unison.

"His manager said- don't send it to her because she is also fired."

Prakash revealed controlling his laughter. The whole group joined him a moment later. I fake-laughed from a distance. I was looking at the group closely. Although the group was enjoying the moment and looked happy, there was a pinch of apprehension hiding behind that laughter- an invisible worry. A worry of getting sacked themselves. The worry of being jobless. The scariest of all worries for a salaried person.

"Kids, these days! So much equality in every field, isn't there?" Ravi, my teammate, commented, watching a group of young boys and girls involved in making rings from their cigarette smoke.

I ignored his sarcasm. I had had enough of such never-ending equality discussions. The best way, the best recipe to turn friends into enemies is this- prejudiced feminism discussions. I had lost enough friends due to such debates which ultimately turned into lifelong ruckus. The best way to not lose an argument is, well, never involve in one.

"What do you think? How much would Kamlesh be earning?" Ravi changed the subject sensing my disinterest. One of the hints to know whether a person is unsatisfied with their job is observing whether they are guess-estimating about other jobs. Ravi seemed to be from that category.

"I think he is earning a lot." I was no different. I was also a part of the above job unsatisfied gang.

"Let's calculate." Ravi had a lot of free time, and now he had a chance to use his analytical skills which were far from what he was doing in the office. "See. I think he sells nearly five hundred cups a day. Let's assume that profit is five per tea. So, he earns around two thousand five hundred."

"Cut the expenses," I asked from the other side of the coin. I remembered Puru and his dream startup.

"The major thing will be the rent. How much would be for, this 5x5? Maybe ten thousand? Or what's your figure?"

"No idea, man. Take at the most fifteen thousand including everything."

"Take maximum twenty. Still, five days a

week, he earns around thirty per month. Not bad, isn't it? Even our freshers can't take home that much."

"And how comfortable his job is." I made a blunt statement. The grass was greener on Kamlesh's side. I wanted to be like Kamlesh. "He seems so satisfied and stress-free, doesn't he?" I continued. "If given a chance, I would happily exchange my job with his." I dreamed.

"Wait. First, his is no job. It's a business. And secondly, who told you Kamlesh would be ready for your offer? He may deny sitting in the AC cage doing nothing meaningful and cursing the destiny. Don't take him for granted."

Sometimes Ravi could be so brutal with his words tearing apart my feelings.

~

Layoffs, firings are the hot topics in the software society. You go to any such bunch-these talks, stories, discussions revolving around layoffs are prominent. And interestingly, most of the people, if not all, have enough intriguing stories to slip out in that genre, some real and some made-up. Nonetheless, they are peculiar and entertaining, even though you feel for that fired stranger. Lalit narrated one such firing case.

"It seemed like a normal Tuesday. Nothing abnormal on the previous day too. Nothing strange on Tuesday till lunch. My friend returned to the desk, and there was an email for an urgent meeting from his manager. In the meeting, he was asked to resign. In no time. The same day. He was dazed. And ask the reasons? No reasons mentioned. I mean, you go to lunch, and you come back, and you go home later, jobless." Lalit was breathless.

"So, what is he doing now?" I was genuinely worried about that fired guy.

"What he could do? He struggled a bit and found another, better job. Then one more again. And then again one more. He was ultimately confused between what to choose. He had three jobs in his pocket. He is now a guy on fire."

"That's good. In fact, better. What else do

you want?" I was relieved because the fired guy was on fire.

"Yeah, exactly. The world is not over if you lose your job. There are a lot of other options, you just need to keep calm and not be furious enough to lose your self-confidence and esteem." Lalit seemed to have analyzed the situation thoroughly and was preparing himself as if he could be the next one. Who knows, he could be.

"Yes, exactly." I submitted my plain response. What else could my worrisome mind think of?

"You know Raghav, we should be prepared."

"Prepared for what?"

"Layoffs. Layoffs are like accidents. You cannot guess who it will happen to and when, and most importantly, why. You are in today; you may be out tomorrow. Who knows? Our organization is no different. Remote is in the US. They press the button, and our channel is switched. Raghav, we should be prepared."

Lalit pondered as if he'd mugged up those lines already. But he had a strong point. He definitely was thoughtful and learned many things by observing others, unlike others who just worry till the devil comes looking for them.

"But what do you mean by preparing? Should we look for other jobs even though we are secure here?" I asked. Lalit was my mentor-figure then.

"I'm not saying look for a job outside. What I'm saying is, observe, explore, think. And no one is secure." He was speaking like a motivational speaker. Although I didn't get what he exactly meant, and I also suspected he didn't understand what he was saying, I looked in his eyes affirmatively.

"Explore your options. Explore what skills you have and how you can earn money from that. Go deep into money-making practices other than jobs. A job is temporary; skills are permanent." Lalit winked.

Those were not just words. That was an alarm. Lalit was not just a man; he was a morning cock.

"Did you find yours?" My Indian mentality was pushing me hard to know what was in his mind before fixing mine on anything.

In a split second, he revealed as if it was his sole intention of striking a conversation.

"I earned ten thousand today through stocks. You too do something."

He winked again and left, tapping my shoulders in consolation. And there I was, standing numb, everything appearing dark in front of me despite the bright morning.

~

The thoughts of being jobless are too tough to be thought of. But not thinking about it at all is, of course, not a solution. We ain't cats.

"Don't worry man. Someone had said- Out of the things we worry about, ninety percent never occur." My friend, who'd switched four jobs in four years, once comforted me.

"Maybe. But who knows if this worry falls in the remaining ten percent?" I was not impressed. "By the way, someone had also said- hope for the best but prepare for the worst." I was quick.

"Okay, it seems your manager is troubling you." He shouted standing two urinals beside me.

'Whose isn't?' My mind spoke.

How can some people be so unripe about corporate toilet etiquettes? Here, you need to talk so silently that the other person needs to conclude only from your lip movements. Toilet walls are too attentive. And there he was, had he raised his tone a little, he must've broken my eardrums.

I looked hastily whether Harish was near anywhere. Fortunately, he was not.

"You know the best trick here?" His volume lowered a little, still not within the range of the protocol.

"What?" I asked.

"Be in formals on random days. Keep your manager wondering whether you are attending interviews and trying for other jobs elsewhere." He said softly.

These worries were not leaving me and not letting me live peacefully. Those imaginary speculations were enough to make me afraid and inwardly upset. I decided to talk to people to see whether they are equally afraid. And if not, if they could give me some assurance. But all in vain. Instead, some started giving me unsolicited advice.

"Afraid? Why are you afraid? If something has to happen; it will happen. Just chill." Chiman, who once emailed to the whole office, 'Sweets in panty' instead of pantry, was encouraging me not to do anything.

"Take calculated risks, no." His further advice.

"Calculated risks? Seems like an oxymoron to me."

"Oxymoron? Is that the exact word for calculated risks?" His ignorance.

"Start with standups. It really stands out. Even if you may not get money, you will surely get a Tinder match." Another friend.

"Not money but a Tinder match? Interesting." I wanted to know the connection.

"Yes, because your match doesn't know you don't earn money. That's the catch." He winked. When I did not laugh, he had another suggestion. "Or better be a Vlogger. They are in high demand. Pack your bag. Forget clothes but don't forget the camcorder. Go anywhere and shoot. I suggest- start with Bhutan. It's easy for us to go there but not to Westerners. And they are your fishes. Big white fishes. Sharks." He winked again.

I called my classmate who used to call me once in a blue moon in his existential crisis, especially in his corporate catastrophe. This time, the tables had turned, and I was the seeker. Before I could ask for anything, he hissed-

"Bro, don't leave the job. I repeat- don't. Do anything, lick but stick."

"But, but.." I tried to intervene.

"How difficult is it to be in your boss's good books? That's the only rule. Don't be in their bad books. Why to play with fire?"

The good thing about him is, not his opinions, but how he keeps me updated with industry jargon and lexicons.

After several such diverse suggestions, I stopped discussing my fears.

"Don't be so open about your fears with others. People take advantage. They think you are too vulnerable and that's not good for you. You may become their laughing stock. I'm telling you this from first hand experience. Find someone sensible who you are comfortable with." My then guru- Lalit aptly advised.

~

The head felt heavy. There was too much chaos for it to handle. There comes a time in life when it becomes difficult to get what the exact problem is, if there's any, and in turn this puzzle adds to the existing chaos. This phase of my life I could relate to such time. For once, I felt I was stuck in the wrong place and at the next I felt when I didn't even know what the right place was, how could I think the job was the wrong place. The intermittent dogma needed to be sorted to seek some peace of mind.

Those were the days when just the thought of going to the office in the morning was enough to turn off the mood. To step out of the bed became a tough task. The Sunday evenings were disastrous.

Would I be happier leaving the job? Would I be happier after switching the job to another? Was that my problem? Or was I thinking of a temporary fix just like my developer colleagues used to do?

Often we make friends by chance. My tea times were matched with that of Mrs. Dayal and surprisingly, we shared similar interest in Indian history. Those coincident tea meets in the pantry and occasional history discussions were enough to make us friends. She was into sales. We both shared one more thing- we couldn't understand each other's exact roles and the work we were doing, and we never cared to discuss about it. Discussing any topic but work was our uncalled protocol. Neither of us fussed about professionals' problems anytime.

"I feel nervous and sad, and surprisingly I don't know exactly why." I told Mrs. Dayal breaking the protocol.

"Hmm, I understand. Melancholy." Thinking sufficiently for half a minute, she said calmly as if she's not into sales but psychiatry.

I appreciate Mrs. Dayal for her rich vocabulary and the perfectly fitting words. But sometimes it gets troublesome to understand her Tharoorian English. Probably meeting sophisticated people all the time made her that way.

"Yes, maybe." I replied and sneakily opened my phone to search for the meaning. "Exactly. Melancholy." I said immediately after completing the search.

"But you know, anyone would hardly be of any help. You yourself need to address it. Give it some time. To solve the problem, we must know the problem in the first place. Introspect. You never know, it may be just a bad feeling and nothing more. We are in the industry where due to the same and mundane, repetitive work, it is not unusual to feel that way. Happens with almost everyone at some point." She smiled assuredly.

"In sales too?"

"Obviously. Sales has some different shit. A sophisticated shit perhaps."

"May be. But, often you get to dine in ultra expensive hotels at the cost of employer's money. Isn't that the biggest boon? Sales is the real business." I chuckled.

What was my worst fear? Getting into depression. It still is. Depression is the place where no one ever wants to visit but I wish if it's a choice not to visit. Why am I bringing the topic of my worst fears? Because I thought it was not impossible for me to be trapped into that bleak state. The pensive sadness could drag me into depression, I was afraid. If I did not address it, I was afraid I could fall into that hole.

"Come on, what are you saying! To me it doesn't look like you have any problem. What is the problem? You won't go into depression. Don't worry. Only rich people go. And you have not even had a heartbreak. You know how much is the probability of that? Zero. So definitely not happening." One ignorant and blatant friend.

"If I listen to you for some more time, I would definitely go." I said. "And an event can happen even with a zero probability. Get your concepts cleared." I was annoyed on his negligence and lack of knowledge on probability.

But it was true at one point- it didn't look like I had any problem from my demeanor. My behaviour with colleagues was hardly any different. I must've looked pleasant to them. Then I realized one thing- we never know how many others are fighting a battle with their innerselves keeping a smile on their faces.

I had a degree. I had a job. For many, having that in itself is a privilege. For many, that may be the perfect life. Perhaps, I was living their dream. From their view, I was settled. From my view, a lot of others were settled. Being settled is a subjective business. But in fact, no one is, unless they've their mind settled in peace.

Was I overreacting on my job trouble? Wasn't it so common these days? Was I making petty problem seem like a serious one?

I felt better after speaking to Mrs. Dayal. After introspection I realized the condition was not as bad as I thought it was. I was not alone. In fact the job exasperation can be termed as a mass-millenial problem these days. And when you know there are more people suffering the same problem as yours, you feel better. But just because they didn't address it and chose to suffer till it gets a routine, are you supposed to do the same? Don't you want to be the change you want to see in your colleagues?

~

"Hey," On some not so exciting Friday

evening when I was busy watching motivational shit on the internet, someone gently tapped my shoulder. It was such a soft and sophisticated touch that I was sure it wasn't my boss who had a habit of peeping at the wrong times. I removed my earphones hastily, and to my utterly pleasant surprise, there was Indu, standing with an ever-constant glowing face and charming smile. Indu, the most beautiful girl in the house and probably in the entire tech park, was standing near me. And a moment back, she, yes, Indu, tapped me.

"Hey Indu," I responded with butterflies chuckling my stomach.

"So?" She raised her eyebrow.

"So?" I copied her.

"Working late today? Don't have any weekend plans?" She asked.

Well, going home and gluing myself to my laptop like I did every day didn't sound like a plan. And, additionally, when someone asks about your plan suggests that probably they have some plan ready for you. Even if I had one, for her I would happily surrender.

"Not really. What about you?" I casually reciprocated with a rare hope.

"Yo! Great. So, you can come with us to a movie, right? Actually, Rakhi canceled at the last moment, and her ticket is spare. I hope you haven't watched Infinity yet."

Even if I had watched it, I could watch it with you infinite times, I wanted to say. I wondered, how honest one could be.

"Infinity? Not yet. When are you planning to leave?"

"Umm, in 5 minutes." She babbled, biting her tongue. "So, you are coming. We are in total six now."

"Seems fine. Let me wrap up and meet you in the parking lot."

"Fine. Or we can leave together. Get ready. I'll just come from the washroom." She disappeared the next moment.

Even after knowing I was invited just to fill the gap and utilize the booked ticket, I was happy. The reason was obvious. I had a chance to spend some time with her after such a long time. The boredom was gone. The excitement was on. Sometimes, I wonder how some special one can lift your mood instantly. My line of thought ended when I saw her approaching me. She returned from the washroom exactly in five minutes as she'd anticipated. How stereotypical I was about them!

Indu and I joined the organization at the same time. We were together in a training batch and were even in the same group for a dummy project. Lucky me. We were thick as thieves, had the perfect bond, superb understanding any project partners could have. We'd given others project-partner goals. But after that, unfortunately, we were split into different teams. There was little I could do to be in her team. I was disheartened. No other guy from our training batch got into her team was the only relief. Eventually and expectedly, the interaction reduced. Timings changed. Work changed. Earlier during training, the whole group used to have tea together, lunch together, copy assignments together, but now that was reduced only to smiles while passing by.

We reached the hall well within time. Fortunately, I didn't know anyone from her team, so she sat beside me. Sensible of her. I could hardly pay any attention to the movie because my mind was still thinking about my unsatisfactory job. Despite a beautiful girl sitting beside me and a popular action movie running in the front, my mind was not letting me come out of the endless thoughts of switching the job. I realized this severe problem needed to be addressed. I needed someone to listen to me, allow me to open up my mind. I needed a sensible listener as Lalit had pointed out. As if I was the Krishna, I needed my Arjuna. During the whole movie, I was thinking whether Indu could be the one? Importantly, the right one? But why would someone like her entertain my problems? And what if she spreads the news? Or probably mocks me behind my back? Still, I thought of taking a chance. I made up my mind and followed my intuition. I don't know why, but I felt she could be the one who would at least listen to me patiently and could probably counsel the way forward to get out of this professional mess. At times, there is no logic or reason why we choose certain people for specific endeavors. It is the inner instinct, and most of the time, it proves perfectly fitting. I decided to go all-in for Indu.

Soon the movie ended and we parted our ways without any discussion-action happening.

The weekend too was no different.

Next Monday, I pinged her as I couldn't afford to lose that golden chance of striking a conversation. After all, I had a solid legitimate reason.

"Indu, how much for Friday's movie?" Without beating around the bush of hi and hellos, I came to the point.

The dawn had begun.

"For you? No. Nothing." She replied immediately as if she was waiting for my message.

'Why? Am I any special to you?' I wanted to hit on her but stopped myself. Instead, I lamely asked,

"Why so?"

"Because I dragged you to join. The movie is on me."

"Okay. Fair enough."

A minute passed. I sensed the conversation could end abruptly, and thus my hopes. With enormous courage, I played my next move.

"In that case, at least let me ask you for a coffee. You know as a courtesy, a free office coffee? In the pantry. Are you free now?" I was acting cool, but in reality, I was shuddering inside. It had been quite a while since I had casually talked to her, or any girl for that matter.

"Haha. Perfect timing. I was about to go for a coffee. How do you know my coffee time? Are you by any way stalking me?" She replied.

I was taken aback. When I was busy thinking about whether to take a step back or push it harder, there came another message from her,

"Chill, chill. No serious business. I'm kidding."

That was a clear green. Definitely, there was some fire left.

"I wish I could, and you don't mind," I pushed.

"That I can't guarantee," she winked.

"Which part?"

"The former one," the winking continued.

"Let's clear this out face to face. I heard the machine generates nice coffee before 11. So, I guess we need to hurry." I was talking nonsense.

"Oh. Is it? Quite new. Anyway, I'm buying this lie. Let's go."

"No need to buy anything. The coffee is free."

The coffee-meet was perfect. We refreshed old memories, and we were both unstoppable in cherishing the past. I wished I could stop the time.

"But Indu, I don't know why we don't meet up often. I mean, we have a lot to talk about."

"And, bitch about," she added instantly.

"Ah, yes yes." I had a good laugh after a long time."Why didn't we talk much after the training?" I asked.

"Mystery to me."

"We can break it," I insisted.

She smiled. Sensing her little discomfort, I asked, further switching the subject,

"I don't have much work. But, you too? We spent more than lunchtime on coffee."

"That's fine. Anyway, my manager is on leave. And, sometimes it is worth it to catch a former project partner," she said, gazing at me.

She was speaking my mind. For a moment I thought, did she get access into my mind?

"Totally worth it," I affirmed. "And a perfect Monday for you."

That night, changing sides, I wondered what had happened that day. Was getting in touch with her that easy? Was that a dream? Was she also in search of someone to bash her problems on? But whatever that was, I felt satisfied as if my intuition had shown me the correct person. What an awesome day that was!

I did not want to lose grip on our reconnect, and from her responses, she reciprocated similar feeling. In subsequent weeks, we conversed frequently, had dozens of coffees and sought the attention of lots of envious colleagues around. The question clearly evident on their faces was, 'Why had she suddenly started hanging out with me?' I had no answer to that, truly because I too had the same question, and I was not in a hurry to get an answer.

Even though I hated to the core to rift the dreamy conversation by my job scuffle, I needed to do that. One evening, I sensed the right time.

"Indu, do you really think you are at the

right place?" I kicked off.

"What do you mean? Being in corporate?"

She sensed immediately what I meant. That's why I always feel that she's the one.

"Yes, yes. I mean, do you really think this is what you want to do, and this work gives you happiness?"

"Um, deep question. Let me take a deep breath." She smiled. A cold minute later, "Frankly, I kind of don't have a one-word answer, a clear answer in terms of yes or no. But this place or this work doesn't bring misery to me. Also, it doesn't give me ultimate happiness. That is also a fact. I know this may seem to be a diplomatic answer, but that's how it is. I don't believe in bashing the industry or the job just because every other person is doing it," she continued.

"Makes some sense." I sighed.

"Choosing software education was my choice and I enjoyed it and now I'm working in the same field, so it's kind of inline for me."

"You know what I'm graduated in? Chemical."

"Yes, I know."

I was surprised.

"I'm glad that you are true to your choices."

She smiled on the compliment and returned to the conversation.

"What are your thoughts? How do you find the job? As you are asking the question, I guess you have issues with this place or the whole industry. Is that it?"

I half smiled. "Well, in contrast to you, I have a one-word answer." I started what I'd been holding in for a long time.

"And I suspect that's- Yes. Yes?"

"Of course yes, you know everything," I giggled.

"That I know. But, tell me something that I don't know yet- your problem. If you want to, of course," she said, sipping her hot coffee.

"Yes, I can go on and on, but this is not the right place. It doesn't look good to crib about the place which places food on your table, does it?" I winked.

~

The very next day on a pleasant evening, I took her to Kamlesh's tea stall- the unofficial hub of office whiners.

"I don't think I'm giving full justice to my skill sets and expertise." I made it clear from my first sentence that it was going to be an intense session.

"By working here?"

"Yes. I mean what I thought I would be doing and what I'm actually doing are poles apart. You are into development. Like you, I'm also hired as a developer you know, but I don't remember when I developed something in the past few quarters."

"What? Really?"

"Yes. Nothing in development. So, I've only developed ill feelings about this job."

"And maybe improved some sense of humor too?" She smiled.

"I wish I could be recognized at least for this sense."

"So, how long has this been going on?"

"Clearly, I don't know when I'm sidelined from the development tasks, but definitely no such work in six months." I said in a small voice.

"Umm, I see." She sipped looking at my frowny face.

And for the next hour, I kept on howling about the problems, and she kept on listening to them patiently. She was not quickly jumping on the conclusions and throwing quick bits of advice. Instead, she chose to be my active audience for most of the time. That's what I like and adore about her.

We frequently had tea outside. Different breaks were spent on different conversations, different topics, different problems. One such fine evening, she brought up the subject all by herself.

"So, is that the main reason- no development work?" Her initiation, her interest in my problems itself made me happy in the first place.

"There is chaos and it is some sort of jigsaw puzzle where some pieces are missing. Frankly I'm not sure. I'm not sure whether development work will make me happy now. In fact, sometimes I question myself- am I in the right field?"

She nodded. "Any preference? If given a chance, where would you work?"

"Maybe somewhere in the creative field. I don't know anything about creatives, but it attracts me and thus I wish to be there someday. But one thing is pretty sure- not in software. Of course not. I'm drained, tired of this. Of this mundane stuff. There is no space for creativity here."

"True to some extent. But again, it's a subjective business." She said keeping her voice down. She looked at me and a moment later, she continued, "People get into the wrong profession. Many of them. They goof up their jobs and so their professional career. The sooner they get that, the better for them. But even with that, what I think is, many folks understand and clearly realize they are running on the wrong road, but the situations, responsibilities make them stay on it- sometimes for their whole life."

"That's absolutely correct, and I agree with it. But even after realizing it, if you are not taking any steps, well, I don't know but…" I couldn't complete the sentence.

"Yes, yes, if you can take steps, well and good. And you must take the chance. But the problem with most people is, they don't even know what steps to take or at least in what direction, what field, what profession." She expressed her inferences.

"So, I am one of them. I too don't know what direction, what field, or what profession," I replied, mocking her words playfully, with a grin.

"Oh, I see. I see." She laughed her heart out.

A minute passed and she started again.

"So tell me seriously, what did you think about it? Did you consult anyone? Everyone has someone whose suggestions we think are always practical and can be followed."

"Not really. Instead, I had some funny encounters to tell you."

"Shoot some."

"People shot lots of advice bullets towards me. You know that guy Munchal who sits just opposite to the pantry door. Beside Pragya?"

"No, I don't remember. I visit Pragya lot of times but never saw anyone beside her."

"Yes, that place is always empty because Munchal is always wandering offering a free consultation. He advised me to be a mattress maker. I mean, to open a small sales unit in the city. He says that's a unique and guaranteed idea to be successful and that's why he doesn't call this venture a startup because startups fail."

"Interesting."

"His uncle is in this mattress business in his hometown, a small scale business. Munchal is highly interested in expanding it. The funny thing I recognized from all such experiences is, people try to enforce their interests on others. Like, someone who is interested in gardening advises you to open a nursery unit even though you are not interested in gardening at all. It's their cheese. It's not my cheese. Everyone should strive for their own cheese."

I was trying to persuade her through my self-help books experience. She did not seem convinced. She is not someone who can be easily manipulated. A tough nut. But that did not stop me. I continued switching towards millennial botheration that was nagging me.

"Sometimes I think today we have a lot of exposure and can see a lot of opportunities, a lot of choices eventually. They are the real culprits. Even though they seem to comfort us, in practical and real sense they make us uncomfortable. Earlier we had a television- one channel, one programme on it and that's all. Our life was sorted. Now, there are tonnes of options and time goes away in deciding what to watch. Similar to it, lots of options to pursue a career in, to settle in, to make us confused- more and more. And this, in turn, increase the probability of choosing the wrong choice maybe?" I was perplexed. Such constant thoughts over a few weeks had made me more flustered. "Don't you think our millennial generation is suffering due to the too-much-options syndrome? And in disguise, we do not even realize it?" That was the longest monologue in a long time I had ever indulged in.

She looked at me. Smiled a bit. "Finished? Let's go back." She insisted.

We left Kamlesh's place and commenced towards the office.

"I will tell you about my experiences. Some personal ones." Now it was her turn.

"Shoot." I copied her response.

She stared at me with a mischievous smile.

"My father will be retiring next year. It is his first and last job. Can you imagine he has worked for more than thirty years in the same banking job? Thirty long years. Although he never complained about the job, I'm sure he too had some bad times there. But he never cared to switch the job or pursue a career in some other field. Why? Maybe because he did not know what opportunities he had. I'm not blaming him, but the time was like that. People hardly knew where they could work happily or at least try to foresee what type of work is better for them, whether their skills would be optimally utilized there. Those people hardly knew about the choices. Isn't today's scene entirely opposite to it? I agree, we have problems but they are of different nature compared to them. In fact, there won't be any time where you won't have problems. They will always be there, just their form gets changed."

She paused. Was it making sense to me? She had more to reveal-

"He sketches really nice. But never had anything published. I'm sure in today's time it is easier than before. We have this liberty. Yes, I agree that the choices make us baffled, but the right choice can make our lives happier. My grandma is excellent in mimicking people. She is excellent to the extent that I knew some of my relatives and how they talk, without ever interacting with them."

"That's funny. And that's fortunate that you need not interact with them."

"But this excellence is known only to us-family and a very few acquaintances. In today's time, if she had explored enough opportunities, she must've been a great artist, we never know. I am not demeaning their way of life, but all I want to say is, if they had choices like we have today, they could've shaped their careers better. Maybe they could have at least given a chance to their skills. Our generation is lucky in that aspect. Isn't it?" She looked at me. "Isn't it?" She repeated.

That made me think deeper. I felt better. After all, everything happening around was not that bad.

Was I too pessimistic about the contemporary situation?

The office was nearer. I wished the stroll never stops and the road never ends.

~

Eventually our friendship grew. The topic list broadened. The chatter timespan widened. During all this time, she tried to let me introspectively find my road, the right path.

Meanwhile, I continued my people-centric observation. I was keenly interested in their happiness at work. During this prolonged activity, I was blessed to stumble upon Girish. Girish is a self-proclaimed human psychology expert.

"Have you seen startup guys? How do they look to you?" He asked.

"Tired maybe?" I was honest.

"Oh God! Okay. But apart from that? Don't they look exciting and enthusiastic?"

"Yeah, sometimes."

"They look tired because they work night and day. They look energetic even though tired." He said something which got me confused for a moment. "They know what work they are doing- for whom, why, what, and how. And that makes them passionate. That makes them happy and satisfied. They work day and night and you work like it's a punishment for you. Why?"

I was about to say 'because of Harish' but he continued without giving me any chance.

"You get tired after working eight hours a day, in that too you take one hour for lunch and a half for tea."

I didn't protest. How to protest against the truth? I oscillated my neck to show my support and that energized him further.

"Humans get happy when they realize the worth of their work. We need to find where our worth lies. This is nothing less than playing a real-life treasure hunt and at the end, you indeed get a treasure."

Every sentence of his was noteworthy. If I had any highlighter, I must've highlighted the entire mouth of Girish, then and there.

Subsequent day, I headed off to take a head-massage. My barber Viju was on my happiness-surveillance list. He has magic in his fingers, those long and lean fingers. The moment he starts thumping those on my head with excessive oil, I feel like I'm in heaven. I wish I could stop the whole world around me except his magic fingers in full motion.

Another reason I feel to visit his saloon is- the positive vibes I get. The atmosphere is always pleasing and entertaining. Viju keeps it that way. His head-to-head conversation with others increase saloon's amusement index. With his experience, he has mastered the art of tickling the right spots of the head by his fingers and of the heart by his conversation. Cricket, Cinema, and Politics, the three entertaining pillars of the country, you ask Viju anything on it and he has his opinions ready.

What I adore about him is- his contented face while working. He is probably the happiest on-job person I've ever encountered. Was the job satisfaction the reason behind that face? Or seeing the satisfied faces of the customer makes him satisfied?

"Do you enjoy all this? This barber business I mean." I asked Viju while he was emptying the oil bottle on my head.

"This is our family business, Sir. So I didn't think of anything else before jumping into it."

"You are damn good at it." I was feeling and liking the cool viscous liquid on my head.

"Probably these skills came as a herediatory gift."

"So, you never thought of doing something else?" After asking this I felt guilty. Was I inducing some poisonous thoughts in his balanced brain?

"If I do something else, who will handle this business? I got this as a ready-made gift. I enjoy it. As long as it pays me enough I don't complain." He was rock solid with his decisions, unlike me.

How different everyone is regarding their jobs? Everyone has their set of situations, responsibilities, and thus the choices.

"Sir, hair fall is too much. Your scalp is visible. Marry soon." He revealed his observation and then the advice.

That gave me a mini heart attack.

"Sir, you are into software job, right?" He changed the subject seeing my discomfort. But his choice of subject was not at all good.

"Yes."

"Don't make any machine which will kill our job." He laughed increasing the motion of his fingers.

"No one can make any machine which will create the fraction of magic your fingers do, Viju. Mark my words."

The office was still the same for me. There was hardly any meaningful work on my plate. Even I did not resist, nor put in an effort to get some real work. I did not complain. I had made peace with the situation. Girish's words were wobbling near my ears like a mosquito. I was in pursuit. On a journey. I needed to work hard to find what work suits me.

The Himalayan Mirage

3

I touched my forehead and could feel the sweat droplets. I cursed my tuxedo. I turned the AC towards me. I looked outside the window, and could not see a single vehicle. I was alone on the empty road, there was a giant elephant walking though. The moment I rested my hands on the steering, the signal turned green. I pressed the accelerator but the car was not moving an inch. I pressed it hard but no luck. The timer of the signal in front of me was stuck just like my car. I remember Karna and his cartwheel. I released the accelerator and pressed the break. I waited for a few seconds, and then I released the break and again pressed the accelerator. I thought it would work after the restart, but it didn't. A car ain't a computer. Frustrated, I got down to check and saw two giant rocks were obstructing the rear wheels. The signal was still green. The counter still showed the number 17. The elephant was still walking. I removed the rocks all by myself. I touched the road and it was smooth as butter. I went inside the car and started it. Suddenly the signal turned red. I broke it. Who cares! My wheels were loving the butterly road and the next minute I was in the office parking.

I looked at my watch and I was on time. In fact before time. Suspicious enough, I looked closely in the watch and all its hands were steady still. My briefcase was lying on the next seat. Although it used to be empty always, I used to carry that. People say- tuxedo when wore with a briefcase makes a man perfect. But that day, it felt too heavy. In fact so heavy that I couldn't lift it. I tried with more efforts to fail again. I touched my forehead and could feel the sweat droplets. I cursed the ventilation of the parking. 'Enough is enough' I said and started the car, reversed it and the next moment we both were out of the parking lot, on the road. I looked in the rearview mirror. I was looking sad. I thought for the reasons but couldn't find any, and that made me sadder.

I was sitting in a camp, a trekker's camp. In search of reasons for my unreasonable sadness, I had reached the Himalayas. The scene was too beautiful to describe. The white snow everywhere your eyes could reach. The people started clicking photos. They all looked cheerful and energetic to me. They had a rush of adrenaline as they climb happily. Where was my adrenaline? There was no trace of it. I was still in my tuxedo. I thought of clicking some photos and upload them to fool people about my eventful life. I took the phone from the pocket. There was some snow on it. I dusted it off and pressed on the front camera. In a moment, I could see white snow, sunshine and a bush. In the picture, everything looked charming except the one thing- Me. I had gray hair, more than the black ones. My stubble was as white as the snow around. My face had wrinkles. For a moment I thought instead of the front camera, I opened some app which was showing me how would I look twenty years later, but disappointedly it was not any app. It was just a front camera showing me a mirror.

I was climbing. I looked around and saw an old Chinese man smiling at me. He looked like a monk.

"Did you sell your Ferrari?" I asked.

"What rubbish!" He screamed at me keeping his smile intact. How was it even possible?

"Okay. But why are you smiling? Am I looking mad to you?"

"No."

"Then?" I touched my forehead and could feel the sweat droplets. The global warming is for real.

" I can solve your problem. You look sad to me."

"Yes, I am sad." I was happy that someone may solve my problem.

"Come here. I will show you where does

happiness lie."

He was standing at the edge of the cliff. The sun was bright. The wind was smooth.

I went near him at the edge. The scene looked serene. He gave me his patented smile. And at the next moment, the very next moment he pushed me. He pushed me from the edge. Oh God! I was in the air falling down. I could still see him on top, still smiling. I was about to hit the ground and experience myself breaking into bits and pieces.

The moment all this could happen, I woke up. I woke up from the disastrous dream with heavy breathing. My heart was thumping loud. What did I see some time back? I touched my forehead and could feel the sweat droplets. I blamed my room's anti-airing design.

I got out of bed immediately. I splashed some water hastily. I looked in the mirror anxiously. Was that dream trying to wake me up? I was a bit relieved because I was not as ugly as I looked in the dream. Would the dream become reality if I don't pursue my happiness?

I decided to address it on priority. I decided to introspect like any other mature adult.

"Oh, you should've died at least." Chiman was not happy with how my dream ended.

"Why so?"

"They say who die in the dream, live for long life in real." He explained.

Chiman is sweet.

When It Struck

4

With many other things, I am equally bad when it comes to gifts, especially birthday ones. Not on the receiving end, of course. I am of that type who is happy to contribute in a group and let the leader decide the gift. But if there is no group, that's difficult for me. It was Indu's birthday, and as expected, I was struggling hard to find her a gift. Even though I wished hard for the perfect gift for her, my mind was blank with ideas. That's how the mind works- it fails miserably when it's needed the most; otherwise, it throws ideas every now and then voluntarily.

"Choose your gifts wisely." Ravi had advised from his not-so-good experiences.

Apparently he had lost many friends due

to his choice of gifts. He lost friendship with Arun to whom he had gifted beautifully crafted ashtray. Arun stopped talking to him because in turn Arun's wife stopped talking to Arun as she'd suspected Arun had cheated and smokes cigarettes without her knowledge. Who gifts ashtray to a nonsmoker? Well, some people like Ravi. "But but, see the art.." Ravi tried to clarify when I asked him about the weird gift.

More to the disaster, he had gifted a mouth freshner to Sunita a month later. Not to surprise, Sunita never talked to him after that.

"She is not talking to me. I didn't even get a chance to smell the mouth freshner I had gifted." Ravi's complain.

The night before Indu's birthday, I was sitting in my room with all the doors of gift-hunting shutdown. I was cursing my empty mind but just cussing was not going to solve the problem. Disappointed, I was on the internet. I logged on to Facebook. Facebook was celebrating my friendships with some strangers. With several filters, my friends looked like strangers to me on Instagram. Other sites were no different, but there was one thing that kept me there. Memes. Dank memes. Hilarious dank memes. Soon, I forgot all about the next day, her birthday, and got submerged in the world of humor- a contemporary world of humor- a world full of creative memes. I visited every other social networking site, and I was greeted with memes- hilarious ones with every type of humor. I could spend days and nights enjoying them, lots and lots of them and still they don't seem to be enough.

I was introduced to this meme world by accident. I accidentally peeked on Puru's screen who was on the bench without any work and was enjoying it fully.

"Nice cartoon," I said.

"It's not that. It's a meme- a new type of humor. Trending these days. They are damn funny, aren't they?"

And thereafter, there was no turning back. I got addicted to its awesomeness. It is an altogether different kind of creativity- a mix of general awareness, wit, humor, sarcasm and what not. I envied meme makers- their skills, their intelligence, their dark humour.

That night, changing sides, an idea emerged. What of a meme-card as a birthday gift? A personal, customized one? I found it to be creative, hilarious, unconventional, and plausible too. The whole night was ahead of me. I felt recharged. I felt energetic. After all, who doesn't like to work on the work he likes? I listed down the topics she discusses, she loves, she talks about unstoppably. I extended the list from studying her Facebook and Instagram. I got a bunch of topics to work on. I summoned my creativity to appear and take hold of my brain, heart, and fingers and work with its full potential. And for the next couple of hours, no one of them disappointed. The piece was almost ready. A great meme-piece. I scrolled the document again, and I was in love with what I had created. A wave of satisfaction, happiness, and achievement gushed within me. I felt proud. I felt confident. The one thing was pretty sure- even if it doesn't amuse Indu, it had already won my heart, and that was noteworthy. You can spread happiness when you are happy in the first place. Such positive, constructive thoughts dashed my mind, and I soon fell asleep- happy and tranquil.

The big day was ahead. With a little modification and finishing touches in the morning, I took the prints. After binding, it looked like a greetbook- a collage of creativity. I could feel the masterpiece. The meme journey of mind-to-paper was so relieving.

The same day there was excessive hustle-and-bustle in the cafeteria.

"Anyone visiting here today?" I asked Shashi who has a stall in the cafeteria and is always well aware about every such event. I could not count on anyone but him for such news.

"There's some meeting I heard. You don't know?" He asked. And then I remembered there was a town hall meeting planned that afternoon.

Town hall meeting is an event where the big players of the company show their faces to the employees. They confirm they're real people and often assure everyone that as far as the organization is concerned, all is well. The employees are interested for that meeting, not because of the top-notch discussion about the company performances and the roadmap, but for the snacks served after it gets over.

The IT team was in full swing that day. It was the most important day of the year for them as they need to ensure every gadget in use work in reality. The stage was set with a big LCD screen for the giants from the US to address. The chairs were cleaned and arranged for the employees to act as if they listen to the speakers. HRs were managing humans so as to get started with the meeting on time. There was rush to occupy the last chairs among the employees. Front chairs were occupied by employees who thought if the CEO could see them, he would remember them and prioritize their promotion.

The meeting started on time and all the gadgets were working fine. Both the departments- HR and IT were heaving a sigh of relief.

"Namaste friends," White CEO could be seen on the big screen. As soon as the crowd heard the Indian word from the foreign mouth, they cheered. He soon started talking about performance and boring numbers. Employees had a good time for a nap. After him, few other folks spoke and then it was a time for question-answer session. After a funny question by the country director, there was a time for some real stuff. A girl raised her hand. I looked at it and the hand felt familiar. She was none other than the birthday girl Indu. In her sweet voice she raised a difficult question. With a comprehensive analysis about the product she was working on, she had gathered the shortcomings and brought to everyone's notice. I was stunned on her qualities- confidence, guts, and the knowledge. She knew the product in and out. She knew what she was contributing in it. Her question made the CEO smirk and he politely passed on the question to the technical head. He answered the question for the next five minutes and praised her for the tactical observation.

The whole town hall episode confirmed how much Indu loved her work and how dedicated she was. She was indeed a star performer and thus her promotion never made anyone surprised.

"I think the company is not in much profit." Chiman said to me.

I was shocked. Was he attentive during the meeting and concluded it from the numbers?

"Why do you think like that?" I asked in a lower voice.

"See there." He screamed pointing towards the snack counter. "Last time there were three items, now it's only Samosa. Also, cold drink is not unlimited it seems."

I was looking for a good time to present Indu the gift and make myself feel relieved. I went up to her desk. I was nervous. I wanted to give her the gift and run home.

"Good job there." I complimented.

"Thank you. You liked my question?"

"You want an answer? Some questions are enough to answer." I said something which I was planning from past five minutes which made Indu confused, and me as well.

And then I presented her my creativity without much hush-hush.

"Take this." I said with my non-excited face.

"What's that?" She asked as if she couldn't guess what it was from its packaging.

"Washing powder for the star of the day." I made a face.

She got my sarcasm. She always does.

"What?" She screamed. "Oh, gift for me?" She seemed surprised. She acted well.

"Don't open it here," I instructed. I knew the gift was praiseworthy but didn't want to influence her with my presence. Also, it could be a little awkward feeling for me, like a teacher checking your answer sheet in front of you.

"It's my gift. It's my property now. I can do anything with it," she naughtily replied.

That night I waited, a little impatiently, as if my exam result was forthcoming. It was late in the night, and I was getting restless with countless thoughts. What if she did get offended? What if not, but the quality of my creativity was just meh? What if she forgot about the card altogether? When I was busy with these thoughts depreciating the mood, my phone beeped. I could hear my heart thumping loudly. A text was waiting for my attention.

"It is MARVELLOUS. THE BEST. THE BEST. Hands down!"

Relief. A big one. I was struggling to find an equally exciting reply.

"I enjoyed it thoroughly. It's just perfect. So much thank you." Her next message.

Now more pressure on me for a more exciting reply.

"Great. Mission accomplished," I responded. No trace of excitement in comparison to hers.

"Wow! I couldn't take my eyes off it. Memes are superb. The collection is great. Up to the point. How well you know me, Raghav!"

"Thank you so much. You know, at one point I was afraid that you might feel offended because this type of humor; you know…you cannot predict how the other person takes it."

"Ah, leave that. I liked it too much. And it is so personal that makes it even more special to me."

"First thing, I was doubtful whether you know this type of thing- these memes. And secondly,"

"Memes on your birthday is the last thing you'd expect." Her next message before I could complete.

"And it is personal, so, you may hate it to the core or like it to the moon," I was justifying.

"The humor is classy. And you know

mister, the dark humor ones where you made fun of me- those are the ones I liked more."

Our emotions were flowing and colliding with each other. We were cutting each other because we had a lot to talk about. The messages were free-flowing. The flattery continued for some more time.

"This huge special thing made me obliged to throw you a treat. Why didn't you ask me for a treat? Just tell me- Why?"

~

We headed off to a decent restaurant in Kormangala on a warm Saturday evening. The place was nice and she was looking gorgeous. But despite of the beautiful atmosphere outside, I was unable to enjoy it fully. The worry of my unsatisfactory job was at the back of my mind, and whenever that thought emerged, it kicked my happiness away.

"Again, coming to the gift stuff, yes, it was great. Thank you for that," she started.

"I know. But I didn't expect you to like it this much."

"Why not? It is of high quality," she complimented.

Unused to such compliments, I responded with an awkward smile.

"Okay, enough praise now, listen." She adjusted her posture and continued. "I thought hard about your skill, and I've got an idea." The reverberance in her voice sounded interesting, and she did seem determined.

"Is it a skill?" I was confused as always. "Anyway, tell me. What idea?"

"My roomie's boyfriend is a freelancer and works in a team with his friends. Do you know what they do?" Her pitch and excitement both went up.

"Android apps?" I blurted immediately. What else could a freelancer do?

"Can you be more creative at least in guessing?" She was not impressed. Android app-lancing is an old school business now.

"Run their own FM channel for corporates?"

"Little more?"

"Collect everyone's tiffin from one office and exchange it with other offices so everyone can have a potluck?"

This time she chuckled.

"No no, not that innovative. Come on." She paused for a second. "Okay, so what they do is the thing you like." She looked at me with hopeful eyes as if I got her clue. "They make memes. Not just as a hobby, but professionally," she revealed, watching my expressionless face.

"What?" There was a change in my expressions; I was indeed surprised.

"Yes, they get paid for creating memes. And they are paid good, not just peanuts."

"Seriously? Tell me more." I could see the hope building inside of me.

"So, I wanted to let you know this. You too can think of pursuing it professionally."

"That I'll definitely think of. But, tell me

more about them."

"Well, as far as I know, they are from different backgrounds and once upon a time, they all were working in corporates."

"Interesting. But, different backgrounds as in?"

"Different fields. Her boyfriend is an MBA; another one is from design and the rest I don't know."

"And they all make memes and money. Great combination."

"Yes, yes, indeed."

"Do they do this full time?"

"Overtime."

"Impressive."

"What I was thinking is, if you want to," she asked, raising her eyebrows, "if, you are okay, if…"

"What if?" I couldn't interpret what her eyebrows were trying to convey. Eyebrows are more powerful than words, she must have thought. But not to me, not to me.

"If you are okay, do you want me to connect you with them? You can talk to them and get some ideas about money making from meme making. What do you say?" She was straight to the point.

"I say- just do it."

~

"Listen," She hopped onto me unexpectedly one fine morning immediately after Kormangala dinner weekend. Whenever she starts with 'listen,' I know it's way too important. "I kind of pitched for you. And they are kind of impressed. Believe me," she continued. She had done the best she could do for me.

"Impressed? Just by your words?" Why would anyone not get impressed by her charm?

"Not just words. They had a glimpse of your work too."

"My work? Which work?"

"My birthday book. That work."

"Did you show that to them?"

"Yes, Sir. So, what? It's completely mine. Why do you look so bothered? Is it because it was personal? But it doesn't have a trace of romance. Right, isn't it?" She asked oscillating her chin.

"Leave that. Let's talk about it later," I responded with a shy smile. "What did they say? Did they like it?" Immediately, I was on the point.

"Yes, of course. If they didn't, I might not have brought up this subject at all."

"Clever." She was. She is.

"So, they liked the idea. They liked the dialogues, the templates, and by all means, the humor. But they said the editing is so immature. There is a huge scope."

"What can a poor man do in a single night! But glad they liked it. Did they say anything else?"

"Good news. The news is that they are

approaching a US firm for getting a contract. They say that there would be a lot of work, and they are short of creative minds. So, you can meet them."

"Fantastic."

~

She coordinated and arranged a casual meet. I insisted that she join, but she refused.

"What will I do there among all you creative minds? Won't I be the odd-woman-out?"

"Actually, we may need a sensible person who can keep the conversation on track. You must know how people fly and get lost when they have ideas."

"You can manage, I know. Go and impress them. I know you can."

"How do you know?"

"I know, I know," she murmured, her eyes down with a little shyness on the face.

We met at a tea stall for the meeting. With three teas down, they explained what they were doing and what their plans were. I was bowled over by their creativity and dedication. Who would have thought that you could be serious about joking! I felt my own spectrum of humour coming out. We hit it off instantly.

Later, Indu couldn't keep calm and was too excited to know what had happened as if it was an appraisal meeting.

"How was it? Cracked the deal? I hope you didn't let my reputation down there." She giggled.

"It was good. Informative."

"I expected you to show some excitement. Let me ask again–How was it?"

"Boys played well."

She laughed. I joined her.

"Come to the point now." She wanted the real stuff.

"They are in need of one more, and they really liked my work. They are ready to take a chance on me."

"Wow. Fantastic. And don't they have any

conditions?"

"They have but the conditions are not tangled, they are plain and direct. The thing I liked about the team is that the guys are way more transparent about what they think. Straightforward."

"Nice. That's commendable. Now tell me about the team. But before that, tell me about something which by now you must be knowing."

"What's that?"

"How do they make money? I mean-how!?" Her eyes were about to come out of the socket.

"That is pretty interesting. I had an idea about the money-making model. But the guys I met, they know the whole and sole of it."

"Of course, they must be. After all, they are into real business. It's their bread and butter. Okay, now tell me."

"There are a lot of ways the money can come. The simplest one is how any social icon earns. Be popular, earn thousands of followers and start advertising through your account. More followers, more money."

"So, these Instagrammers do that a lot, right?"

"Yes, exactly. That's the simplest and pretty straightforward."

"And, how are you guys planning to go about it?"

"Well, how they are planning is, they won't post the stuff directly by their account. They will create stuff, a hell lot of it, and hand it over to the client company which is nothing but an advertising firm which further has their clients. These clients are of diverse backgrounds and have global reach. So, the material they need is also of a diverse nature."

"Diverse as in?"

"Of every field- film industry, technology advances, sports, arts, politics, history and a lot more."

"And how that will be used?"

"The clients will use their influencer accounts to indirectly publicize their products. It's a smart way of publicity. In another way, if their influencers garnish some more followers-thousands, let's assume because of our material, they can utilize this follower strength in the future."

"Will there be only memes?"

"Not exactly. But, majorly, yes, memes."

"What type of products do they make where your memes will be used?"

"Mainly they are knick-knacks."

"What's that? It seems like you learned a lot of fancy stuff. Huh?"

"Yes," I laughed. "Knick-knacks are small household products, and many times are worthless. Like mobile holders, bathroom soap holder, fridge magnets. Things which are just for fancy, not for real use."

"But creativity reflects from them."

"Yes. And also, in a big market for t-shirts

and hoodies. Witty one-liners are trending on these tops. There lies a huge scope. Current affairs and memes on that, people like to have on their clothes."

"In the hope that others will assume the guy is up to date with a dark sense of humor."

"Maybe. But, let that be. I bless those. They are running the business." I winked.

"So, this will be displayed only over the internet?"

"This covers all–newspaper advertising, social media, roadside posters, movie screening ads."

"Aha, I understand."

I was waiting for her further questions.

"Create something meaningful. Those movie screening ads are so pathetic."

"Point noted. I'll convey." I smiled.

"So, that's it? Anything more?"

"And also, advertisements to bash their competitors."

She was silent for a clear half minute. She took out her water bottle and took a sip. I thought she was done, but I was wrong.

"What is their team like? Tell me more." She insisted.

I had no choice. "There are only four. Aman, your roomie's boyfriend, is not just MBA. He is an MBA from IIM. It's a really big thing. He was in investment banking. Earning tons of money. Another guy, Vinod, is their design specialist- a graduate from NID. He didn't join a big design firm and struggled a bit on his own. Another one is Aman's classmate and friend who claims Aman convinced him to leave his job and work on Aman's passion."

She laughed. "Yes, some friends are evil, and they are way better at convincing others. And the fourth one?"

'Are you one of those evil ones?' I wanted to ask.

"I don't clearly remember his name, but he is from economics background and way more knowledgeable in Indian politics. He didn't come to the meeting."

"And what would you be doing? Anything in mind?"

"They must have. As I am from IT, they must be expecting something in the software field. Also, India is the biggest market for such work, and software folks really like the jokes on themselves. Isn't it? Don't you like jokes about your profession?"

"Yes, yes, go on. Make jokes on me, my work, my regime. You are a free bird. And I know, and I've seen how much you know in-and-out about IT."

"They asked me to make more and send it to them. They want that to be included in their portfolio. So, I need to work now."

"Ah, that won't be tough for you. So, you can be the fifth Pandav right?"

I smiled. The crooked smile was enough to show my dilemma. She sensed it.

"What is the problem then?"

"It's not a problem. It's actually an

opportunity for me to get out of the shit, but you know what? I am scared. The work they are expecting is huge. Everyone needs to work their asses off. They are working full-time on that. For me, they asked whether I'd be working full-time. It's not that they have this stringent condition, but they expect more time invested, of course for all the valid reasons."

"You are scared of the work or the full-time commitment?"

"Of course, this full-time thing. The work will be a lot, no doubt, but it will be fun. It will be a lot of fun. I remember how much I enjoyed making your gift. The work is not a problem. The problem is my confusion. I don't understand why I'm so confused. Earlier, I was struggling hard to realize what could make me happy, what I shall work on to make me feel valued and satisfied. And now, when I think I know what it is and even have the opportunity, I am getting scared. There should not be a reason to get scared, should there be? But, honestly, I am."

"Hold on, hold on. Relax. And this is normal. There is nothing unusual about getting confused about career choices. This is really a big thing. Get yourself some time. Chill. Don't be so impulsive. The world is not ending tomorrow. Is it?" She asked with her big eyes.

That got me giggling.

"Yes, today is not 20th December 2012."

She stared hard at me.

"Oho! Humor is back," she said, sweet as pie, after a second.

I always feel she catches my attempts of indirect humour.

"Okay, so tell me, did you visit their office?"

I stared hard at her.

"What?" She reciprocated.

I continued my glare. This time harder.

"Oh, do they have an office in the first place?"

"Now this is a legitimate question. And the answer is No."

"So, the house is the workplace?"

"Yes. They have a flat in Malleshwaram and they work from there."

"Sofa cum bed types?" She beamed from ear to ear. I did not laugh. "Sorry, sorry, tell me more. Don't mind my sofa-cum-bed jokes."

How could I mind?

"So, you know what their infrastructure is?"

"Their wit?"

She definitely is witty.

"Ah! Good one. Yes, but apart from that, they have subscriptions. Subscriptions of all types- Magazines, Netflix, Prime, Hotstar. You name it, and they have it. They say- you never know from where may you get inspiration, an idea. So why to take a chance, take the subscription."

"Hmm, you never know."

"Yes, you never know."

"If they watch programs all the time, that's

enjoyment." She seemed envious.

"Enjoyment-cum-work to be precise. And not only that, they go for stand up comedy shows often, art exhibitions sometimes, and comic cons whenever in town. And of course, it is a part of the work. The inspiration and content wait for you at the places you least expect it." I winked.

"Yes, I agree and after all, you never know..."

"You know they go to crowded places regularly because who gives better content than people?"

"So, we the people are your guinea pigs? How inhuman!" She said with a funny aggravated face.

"Not like that. But, observation is important. We must know what's going on around us because people connect more to what they see around."

"Makes sense. And, you never know..." She blinked.

I realised she was in a different mood.

"But you know what?"

"What?"

"Well leave it," I said not looking at her.

"I guess a meme-maker don't want to get murdered even before becoming a meme-maker. Isn't it, meme-maker?"

"Those guys think we are a couple," I improvised looking straight into her beautiful dark brown eyes.

~

The next few days were a ruckus of emotions- a rollercoaster of excitement, anxiety, joy, and fear. At one point, the opportunity looked golden and at the next, a deadlier. At one point, the dull job seemed just a bad phase and could be resolved, and at the next, I felt disgusted to be trapped in a comfort zone. The haunting questions were endless. But the basic one remained the same- to go or not to go? I could have talked with many people, but that could hardly be of any help. People throw a free bit of advice like litter because that's not their problem. And I don't blame them for that because if even I am asked to advise, I may do the same.

Even after knowing all this, I couldn't hold the urge to take the advice of a person who started this. When I asked her what to do, she had a very mature response. She told me to take complete ownership of the decision, whatever it may be, and the consequences coming with it.

"You ask people, and they will throw opinions as per their thought processes, ideologies. What about your ideologies? Your plans? And as you said- it's not their cheese. It's damn freaking yours! You know yourself better than them. And also, whatever happens, you have to live with it, not them. They will hardly be affected by it. You decide and thrive hard to make that decision successful. That's it." She spoke breathlessly as if she had this response ready. That made complete sense but made the light atmosphere a bit serious.

It made me happier that she remembered and even quoted my cheesy lines.

A minute later, I looked straight into her eyes. “Were you on any motivational marathon yesterday, Indu?” I got her point, so there was no point in pushing the ongoing serious discussion further.

“Oh, come on.” She laughed hard. Her honest laugh on my humor made me more inclined to join the team.

“And you know what they say in our industry?”

“What? Tell me.” She is always hungry for new things.

“There is always a beautiful woman behind every successful meme maker.” My heart pace could’ve won the marathon.

She looked at me for a moment. “Oh, calling me beautiful on my face. Improvement. Keep it up.” Lips slightly pursed and drawn into a playful smile, she cheered.

~

Although I was inclined to join the meme-team, I was not fully convinced about leaving the job and working full-time with them. After all, it was the biggest decision I needed to take, and my savvy head was warning me not to take any steps in haste. When I was getting thoughts of playing easy and slowly, I got to know that the meme-team was planning to kickstart their work, and there was no change in their schedule.

"I think they are firm on their plan, and if not you, someone else or just the four of them would do it, but they won't wait for anyone." Indu warned me one day. I realized where her inclination was.

In the same week, there was a hot topic trending in the office- the bonus.

"The company is in huge profit this year. And also, I heard many projects are lined up. So, a huge bonus this year." Puru was confident.

"Is it confirmed?"

"I heard Suresh tell them in their team's

quarterly lunch yesterday." He had proof.

That was excellent news, but that didn't make me optimally happy. Instead, it added to my confusion. My pendulum tilted more to continue the job, and I hated that. Sometimes, I wonder why good news comes at incorrect times. To make the situation worse, the deadline of conveying my decision to the team was approaching. My decision of not taking any decision makes me hate myself sometimes.

The news of the hefty bonus spread like wildfire, and it started showing an immediate effect- excited people all around. People started speaking of positivity, technology and what not. The immediate shift of their attitude towards their employer was unforeseen. Days went by, and in between these happy people, my confused soul couldn't decide anything, and so, by default, my decision to the team went as not interested. And as if it was not sufficient to make me disappointed on myself, Indu stopped taking an interest.

When I interrogated her, she said, "I am not disappointed in your decision to continue the job as your job might now be pleasing you after the news of the hefty bonus. That is fine. But what surprises me is that you couldn't decide on what to choose, and not for others, for yourself. Damn. Maybe, you want someone else to come and make the decision for you, and later, if that doesn't work out, you can blame them for your failure. That is not fine."

Her words struck me hard, like a sword clenching my body. She left immediately, but her words remained with me. Her every word was right, though not pleasing to perceive. And then I realized what I was left with. Only two things: the job I didn't like and the opportunity to do the work I did like which I missed, out of which the latter could haunt me for a lifetime.

~

One not so welcoming Monday afternoon, Harish called for a team meeting.

"There is a new client coming up," he announced with a smile. "And from immediate effect, we need to start working on it." His smile disappeared.

He was all prepared with his plan- who would drive the project and who does what. He calmly disclosed the distribution of work, and to my surprise, there was hardly any substantial work for me, despite being a mid-senior in the team. I was supposed to document everything- go to and fro when there are changes in the design and follow up on my juniors. This was light years away from what any software developer must do.

That must've made me upset and frustrated, but it had the exact opposite effect. I felt liberated. I felt clear and composed. I returned to my desk with a smile. I laughed how I fooled myself out of the hefty bonus news. The meeting helped me to make a decision- a firm one this time. I thanked God and Harish for resolving my dilemma.

Without wasting any more time, I immediately called Aman to see if there was still any chance left. After some embarrassing talk when I again expressed my interest to work, I could see hope in his words.

"Unfortunately, we lost the US client for

which we had a talk. But the good news is, we have another one, and we hope we can grab the spot there. We are preparing a tentative plan to present it before them. If the plan works to make them happy, we need to start working immediately. Raghav, I understand your situation, but you know our meeting is due in a week, and we are positive on that. If we crack it, we need to start the work from the next day. Also, the condition with this client is they need a full-time working team to expedite the delivery. So, if you want to join, you may need to- well, leave the job." A moment later he continued, "But I'm not sure if you can do that even if you are willing to. What is your notice period by the way?"

"It's two months."

"Any negotiations? How are your relations with your manager and HR?"

"Umm, worse than Indo-Pak maybe." I chuckled.

"Awesome." He laughed sarcastically.

"Let me see what I can do," I assured.

"Let me know as soon as possible because I need to tweak the plan accordingly. Sorry, but can you let me know by tomorrow?"

I could visualize the moment as do-or-die, and I chose to do.

"Count me in." Determined, I confirmed.

The next call went automatically to Indu.

~

On a dinner table, before she could start with the starter, I started. "I am resigning." I was as cold as the soup in front of me. "I couldn't care less for the job now."

"Really? When did this happen?" That made her attentive instantly.

And I spit all out what had happened the whole day.

"But, when will you leave? And what about the notice period?"

"As early as possible. Next week probably. And well, about the notice period, I don't know. I am really not sure," I sputtered.

"How do you connect with Suchi?"

"Not so good. Really not so good since that referral recruitment drive. She was upset with me when my friend didn't join. What was he supposed to do? They put something else in his offer letter than what was decided in the interview."

"Then, she won't spare you. They'll insist that you complete the notice period."

"Yeah, they'll make me obligatory. I am thinking of buying that out. What max can happen? Two months' salary. It has to be okay against my confused mind which took so long to decide." I was not confused anymore; I was as clear as water.

"Wow. I am impressed with your determination. Good job."

The main course went silent. I indulged in my thoughts, and she too must be in the most obvious question. I was waiting when she hesitantly asked that. She didn't let me wait for long.

"Everything looks okay, but I need to ask you one thing."

"I know, what's that."

"So, why are you waiting. Tell me everything." She was in her typical info-starved mode.

"Money. Money. God damn money. Everything surrounds money, doesn't it?" I laughed.

"Yes, start now." She was hardly interested in knowing how money is secondary.

"Now it'll be on a performance basis. The clients have such a contract that it will pay X amount of money and based on the performance of the product, the next batch of payment comes. The more the public like it, the more money."

"So, you are not going to tell me exactly. At least tell me that directly. It's fine if you don't want to reveal." She was a bit irritated by my elusive explanation.

"The thing is, I am also not clear on that." I was honest and as puzzled as her regarding the money.

"Okay, so simplifying it some more, the money can be distributed among ourselves based on how everyone's work performed outside and how it got the attention of the public. And that's it. A bare minimum amount for sure for everyone and the rest on the performance. But the money is not that bad initially. If the work really strikes, there is no limit." I came up with a better version, and she found it digestible.

"You'll be uncle Scrooge with a sea of money, isn't it?" She was way too optimistic and exaggerative.

"Only Scrooge knows." I am a man with uncertainty. "But you know what? Really, I am not doing this for money. I want to live carefree, do what I think I can do better. If that's fun, and I'm able to provide food on the table, I can compromise on everything. At least, let me give myself a chance. Why should I be so harsh on my skills and interests." I should deliver self-help lectures I thought.

"Yes, go ahead. And if you are happy, I am the second most happy person after you." She shyly looked at me. I couldn't match her eyes, but my blush was evident to her.

"And as we are discussing money, have you heard of this axiom? Bad news travels fast and bonus rumors faster?"

"No," I said clearing my plate and the next moment, I realised she'd said something unusual. "And what? Bonus news is a rumor?" I was happily surprised.

"Yes, a big hoax. I'm doubtful whether we would get anything, leave aside the fat one," she said, handing over the card to the waiter.

"Indu, don't. I invited you. It's my treat. My resignation treat." I protested.

"Let me pay, you jobless fellow. And take me to some five-star when you become Uncle Scrooge. That treat is pending on you. When is that planned? Tell me that."

I laughed. I didn't protest. Who doesn't like a free meal?

Today

5

I am jobless and that's the reality. It's 6 o'clock in the morning, and I'm all awake. Apparently, if you don't have any work, you wake up early. It's been quite a while since I felt the morning so pleasant. I decided to make optimal use of its pleasantness. I jogged, read a newspaper, had a luxurious bath and still had plenty of morning left. I went ahead and made myself cardamom mixed ginger tea- in a perfect proportion, just the way I like. With a hot cup and cold head, I went to the balcony to enjoy it fully. In the cool breeze, I could see a ray of sunshine just like the new choice I had made. The hustle and bustle were clearly visible on the life beneath me. In no time, I caught a glimpse of a suited guy rushing to catch a cab. Although leaving a job was almost my choice to take a chance, a part of me still missed something about it. But that's what memories do; they haunt you the more you try to turn a blind eye to them.

Even though I eminently hope, this is not a cinema or a cliched fiction to make me an overnight success. I am quite aware of that and was aware when I intentionally fell into it. The road is foggy- unclear for me to see what is there in store. I am not sure whether I'll be a successful meme maker or unsuccessful enough to make a meme of myself with my weird career choices. Many people might ask why I chose this; even I sometimes get skeptical and unintentionally ask myself the same question. I distinctly remember a quote from a gentleman whose name I forgot. 'Give yourself a fair chance.' And that's what I am following. Even though I may fail at what I'm planning, at least ten years down the line, I won't say, 'At least I should have tried that.' Failing is okay, regret is more painful. And, well, if I succeed, I'm all set for the interviews and won't have any aforesaid thoughts.

My mind got busy in speculating reactions people would throw at me when they'll get to know about my job-adventure. Would they react the same on my face and behind my back? Let me guess. People may term it as a bold step and assure me success on my face for sure. And behind my back, would they term it a foolish step and worry about my earnings? Would my family react any different? Perhaps the exact opposite? But the least benefit I have from all this episode is- stories to tell to my kids. After all, they have all the right to know how their father chose the path less travelled. I would be happy to spice it up a bit to prove myself a hero. I would be happier if Indu would agree to be the mother to them.

The weather was superb- a perfect blend of lucent sunshine and a brisk wind. I couldn't remember the last time I felt Bangalore weather so refreshing. It seems you need not go to Nandi Hills for witnessing the delightful morning. If you are happy and content from inside, it always feels Nandi Hills outside. Maybe that's why the ultimate aim of life is achieving that state- that peace, that satisfaction, that tranquility of mind. Maybe that is the reason why modern success is measured by the inner peace and Master Shifu was stressing on it.

I was making a to-do list for the day. That was a habit; the only difference was technical tasks replaced by personal undertakings. I thought of starting off with never-before-done things. But apparently, that had already been started with me being jobless for the first time or never before. 'Jobless' is a difficult word to perceive. It haunts. Why is making ourselves happy not considered a job that we all shall serve on priority?

I decided to watch a movie in the afternoon. Let me be on a solo-date, I thought. Let me enjoy the best ever company, I wished. Also, I was interested to know how these cinema halls look on weekday afternoons. I wanted to confirm whether was it really a couple's playground. Besides, observing people was a part of my new stint. Maybe I would get some ideas to create memes from that? Maybe I can pay for a normal ticket and sit on the recliner seat once the lights go off?

When I was about to finish my tea, the phone rang. Surprisingly, it was Harish. The stream of thoughts gushed my mind. Why is he calling me now? My heart skipped a beat. Does any formality still persist? But in that case, Suchi would have called. Did I miss something important on my desk? Why the hell would he care about that? Is he proposing a new role for me with a revised salary, an onsite opportunity, and a separate posh cabin to sit in? Ahh, no way. And then suddenly it struck me. In the haste of firing and sending me home immediately, Harish forgot to ask me for a handover. The only task from the past two months I had was to take care of the client's server. Only I was given access to it with my credentials. I knew Harish would have a tough time in resolving the issue. After some time, he would eventually get hold of the situation, that too I knew. But, for that some time, at least for a few moments, let him suffer and let me enjoy. Let the tables be turned, for a change. I guess that's what they call malicious pleasure. Everything appeared more pleasant, even the tea- mild by now- tasted better.

I didn't pick up the call. I looked all around. It felt refreshing as if some serene happiness of a breeze caressed my inner self. I watched the sun peek through the clouds and hoped to find peace amidst the chaos. Ultimately, that's what we seek, isn't it?

~ The beginning ~

"Some failure in life is inevitable. It is impossible to live without failing at something, unless you live so cautiously that you might as well not have lived at all—in which case, you fail by default."

- J. K. Rowling